# THE MARVEL
# OF LIFE

Words in *italics* in the main
text (*or in* Roman *type in
the captions*) are explained
in the Index and glossary at
the book.

A Cherrytree Book

Adapted by A S Publishing
from *LA MARAVILLA DE LA VIDA*
by Dr Mercè Parramón
illustrated by Francisco Redondo
© Parramón Ediciones, S.A.- 1992

This edition first published 1993
by Cherrytree Press Ltd
a subsidiary of
The Chivers Company Ltd
Windsor Bridge Road
Bath, Avon BA2 3AX

© Cherrytree Press Ltd 1993

British Library Cataloguing in Publication Data

Marvel of Life.- (Invisible World Series)
I. Halton, France II. Series
612

ISBN 0-7451-5206-6

Reprinted 1995, 1997

Typeset by Dorchester Typesetting, Dorset
Printed in Spain

INVISIBLE WORLD

# THE MARVEL
# OF LIFE

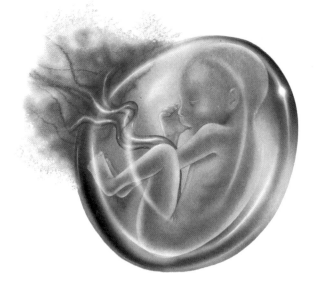

Edited by
Frances Halton

CHERRYTREE BOOKS

# The beginning of life

Where do we come from? All of us – like almost all animals – began life as a single cell, which divided over and over again to develop into a complete new person. Every cell in your body is descended from that first cell; and it was made when two special *sex cells*, one from each of your parents, joined together.

In birds and many other egg-laying animals, most of the development takes place outside the mother's body. The bird lays an egg, and the young develops inside the shell until it is ready to hatch. The young of other animals, such as elephants, mice and humans, develop inside the mother until they are ready to be born. The process by which living things give life and birth is called *reproduction*.

The first step in the process of reproduction is the joining of the two special sex cells. One of these comes from the father, the other comes from the mother. The male's sex cell is called a *spermatozoon*, or *sperm* for short. The female's is called an *ovum* (plural *ova*), or egg. Reproduction begins when a sperm joins with an ovum to make a single new cell called a *zygote*. This process is called fertilization.

When it is fertilized the zygote is smaller than the head of a pin, but it contains all the information necessary for producing a new being: the colour of the hair, the length of the leg the correct number of teeth, the colour and shape of the eyes, the shape of the nose and so on. This information is passed on to every one of the cells in the new being. The information is carried by *chromosomes* in the *nucleus* of the cell.

*A new life is beginning. The miracle of life depends upon two tiny cells. The small diagram (below right) shows clearly what is happening in the big picture. Millions of sperm (1) struggle to reach a single egg, or ovum (2). Only one of them (3) will make its way into the egg and fertilize it. The fertilized egg will then divide and develop inside the mother's body.*

A

B

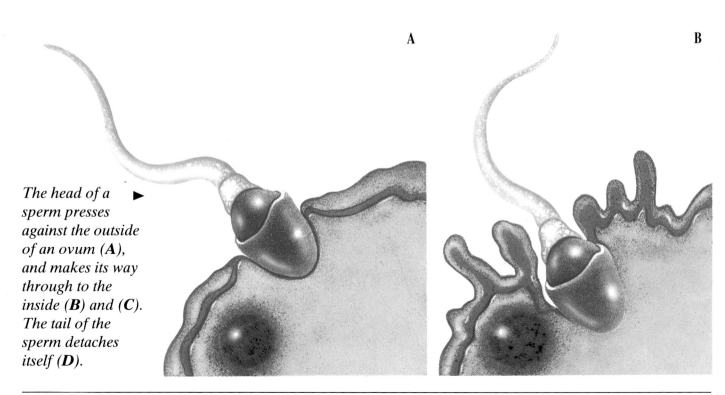

*The head of a* ▶ *sperm presses against the outside of an ovum (A), and makes its way through to the inside (B) and (C). The tail of the sperm detaches itself (D).*

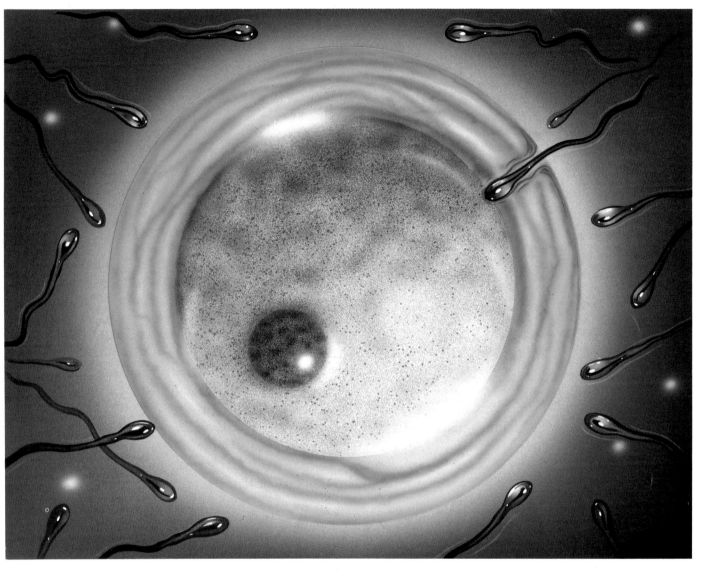

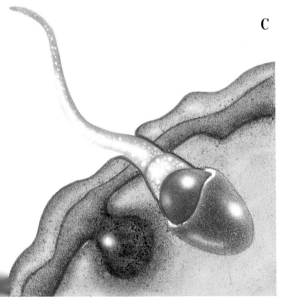

C

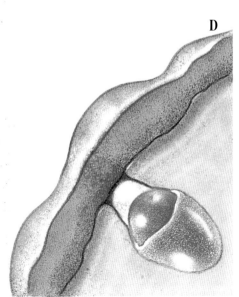

D

# The female reproductive system

*A woman's reproductive organs (red) are inside her* ▼ *abdomen, in the space between the hip bones which is called the pelvis.*

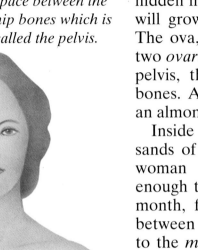

A woman's reproductive system is hidden inside her *abdomen*; her baby will grow in safety inside her body. The ova, or eggs, are formed in her two *ovaries*. These are situated in her pelvis, the region between the hip bones. An ovary is rather similar to an almond in shape and size.

Inside each ovary are many thousands of tiny immature egg cells. A woman is born with more than enough to last her all her life. Every month, from *puberty* (which occurs between the ages of about 11 and 14) to the *menopause* (from about 45 to 55), one or more of these cells matures into an ovum. This process is controlled by a *hormone* called *oestrogen*, which is produced in the ovaries. Oestrogen also controls the development of the *sex characteristics* which make women different from men.

Each month a mature ovum leaves its ovary and passes into one of the *Fallopian tubes,* or *oviducts,* which connect each ovary to the *womb*, or *uterus.* This is a hollow organ with muscular walls, which lies in the middle of the woman's pelvis. It is roughly the shape and size of a small pear. When an ovum is fertilized it attaches itself to the wall of the uterus and grows there, taking nourishment from its mother, until it is ready to be born 9 months later.

The lower end of the uterus leads to the *vagina*, a canal about 7 to 9 centimetres long which connects the uterus with the outside of the body.

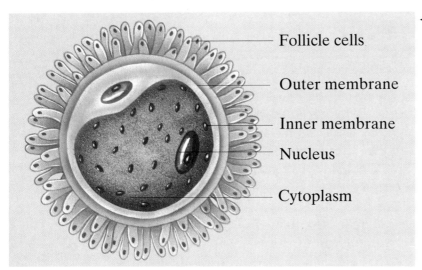

Follicle cells

Outer membrane

Inner membrane

Nucleus

Cytoplasm

◀ *This is what an ovum looks like under a microscope. It is surrounded by frond-like* follicle *cells that help it move. Two tough membranes protect the inside which is made of a jelly-like substance called cytoplasm. The nucleus is the control centre of the cell.*

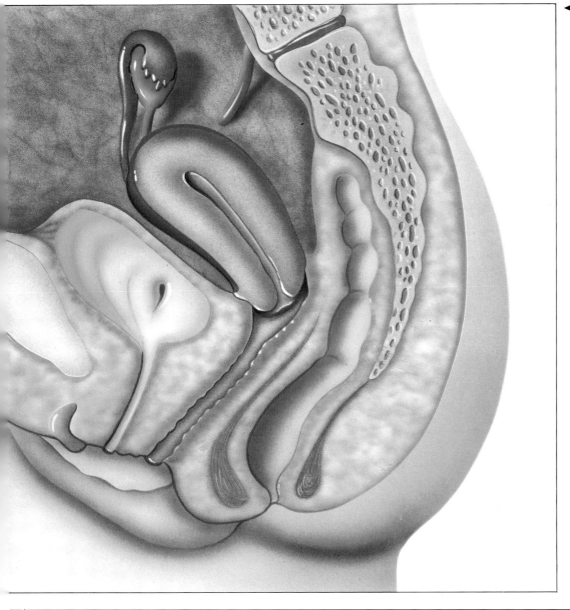

◀ *The female reproductive system. Its parts are numbered in the small diagram (above). The almond-shaped ovary (1) is partly covered by the fringed, trumpet-shaped end of the Fallopian tube (2), or oviduct. The oviduct leads to the uterus (3), where the ovum will grow if it is fertilized. The vagina (4) connects the uterus to the outside of the body. The female reproductive organs lie just behind, and slightly above, the bladder (5).*

# The male reproductive system

*A man's* penis *and* scrotum *are outside his body. This keeps his testicles slightly* ▼ *cooler than the rest of his body, which is necessary for the production of healthy sperm.*

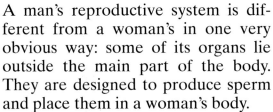

A man's reproductive system is different from a woman's in one very obvious way: some of its organs lie outside the main part of the body. They are designed to produce sperm and place them in a woman's body.

The sperm are formed in the testicles. These are two *glands* which lie on the outside of the body, in a pouch of skin called the scrotum. Each testicle contains a large number of tubes called <u>*seminiferous tubules*</u>, in which the sperm are formed. Between these tubes are cells which produce the hormone *testosterone*. This controls the male reproductive system and the development of the sex characteristics that make men different from women.

Sperm are stored in the testicles in a coiled tube called the *epididymis*. From there, they make their way out of the body through a long tube called the *vas deferens* to the *urethra*. They are mixed with a liquid called seminal fluid, which is made by the *prostate gland* and the seminal vesicles, to form *semen*. There are usually 100 to 200 million sperm in a cubic centimetre of semen!

The urethra is a duct leading to the outside of the body through the penis. It carries semen, and also urine from the bladder, but never at the same time. When a man is going to eject semen, his penis becomes hard and stiff, and the tube from the bladder is shut off. The penis deposits the semen containing the sperm inside the woman's vagina.

*The external organs of the male reproductive system are the penis (**1**), and the scrotum (**2**) containing the testicles. In each testicle is a mass of seminiferous tubules, where the sperm are formed. The vas deferens loops around the bladder (**3**), inside the pelvis. The prostate gland (**4**), below the bladder, secretes seminal fluid with which the sperm mix to form semen. The urethra (**5**) has two functions; at different times it takes either semen or urine from the bladder through the penis and out of the body.*

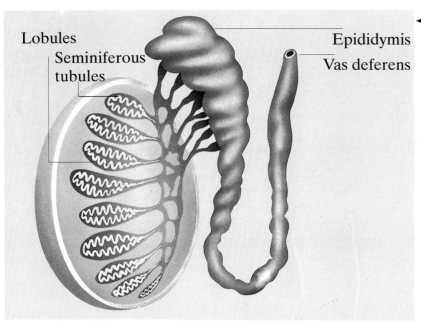

Lobules
Seminiferous
tubules

Epididymis
Vas deferens

◄ *Inside each testicle is a mass of seminiferous tubules. Here the sperm are produced. The network of tubes leads to the epididymis where the sperm are stored. They leave the body by way of the vas deferens which connects with the urethra close to the prostate gland.*

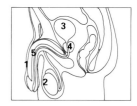

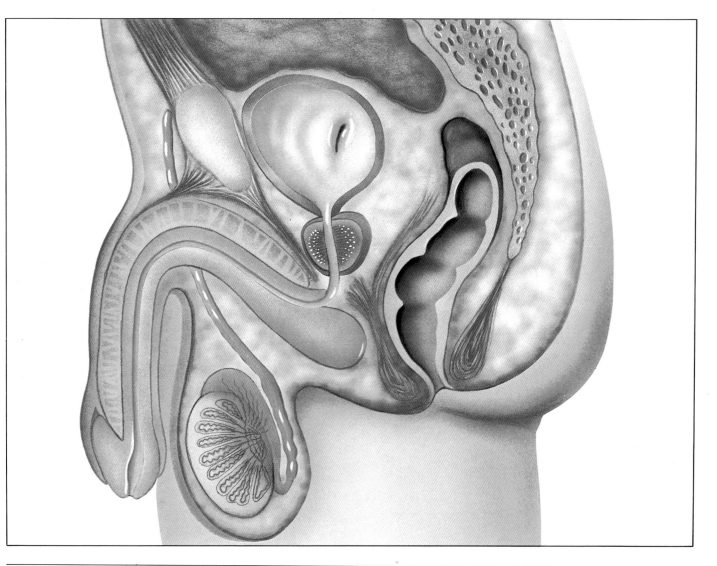

# Growing up

The way in which we grow and develop is controlled by hormones produced in our *endocrine glands*. These glands include the ovaries in a woman and a man's testicles.

When we are children, there is not much difference between girls and boys, apart from the obvious difference that boys have a penis and scrotum. But during puberty a spurt of growth takes place, and boys and girls begin to develop in different ways. Puberty occurs in girls between about 11 and 14, and in boys a little later (between about 14 and 16). At this time, their endocrine glands are producing large amounts of hormones.

The most obvious changes that take place in a girl's body during puberty are the growth of her breasts, the growth of hair under her arms and between her legs, and the beginning of *menstruation*.

Menstruation – also known as the monthly period – is the loss of blood through the vagina. This lasts for about five days, and begins every 28 days. It is part of a woman's complicated reproductive cycle. As we know, each month an ovum in one of her ovaries matures. This passes out of the ovary into the oviduct, and down to the uterus. Meanwhile hormones produced by the ovary cause the cells lining the uterus – the *endometrium* – to grow thick with tissue rich in blood vessels. It is getting ready to take in a fertilized ovum. If the ovum is not fertilized the hormone production changes. The extra lining of the uterus breaks down and together with blood from little broken blood vessels passes out of the body through the vagina.

When a boy reaches puberty, his shoulders and chest broaden, and his skin becomes coarser. His voice grows deeper, and hair appears under his arms, on his face, and around his penis. His sex organs grow bigger, and finally his testicles begin to produce sperm.

*A woman's reproductive cycle. The first diagram shows* ovulation *(A), when an ovum which has matured in the ovary passes out of its follicle and into the oviduct. The ovum makes its way along the oviduct (B & C), while the lining of the uterus grows thicker. This is the time of the month when a woman is most fertile. When the ovum reaches the uterus it may have been fertilized. If it has not been fertilized, the thick lining breaks down and menstruation begins (D).* ▼

A                    B

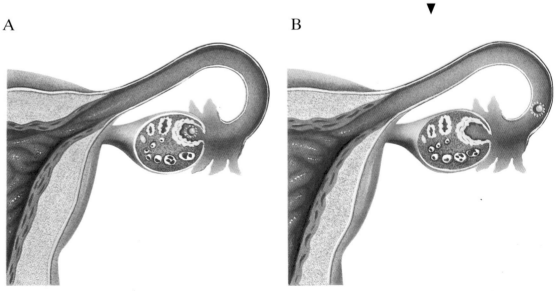

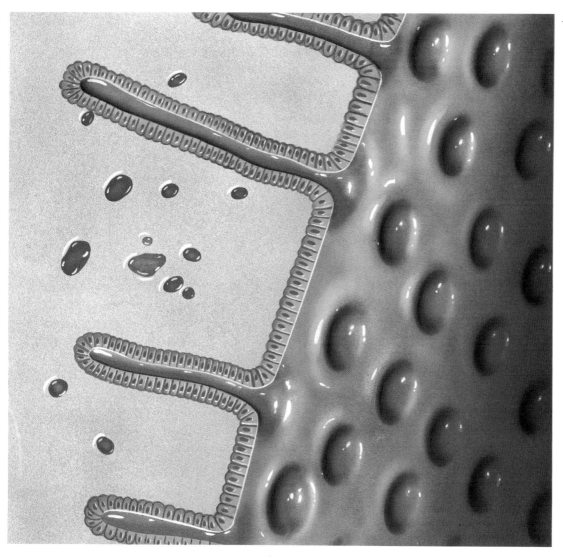

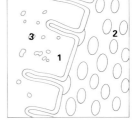

◄ *A close-up picture of part of the uterus during menstruation. The thickened layer of the endometrium (1) is being shed, because it has no fertilized ovum to look after. Together with some blood (3) from tiny broken blood vessels, it flows out of the body through the vagina. The muscular layer of the uterus (2) remains unchanged.*

C

D

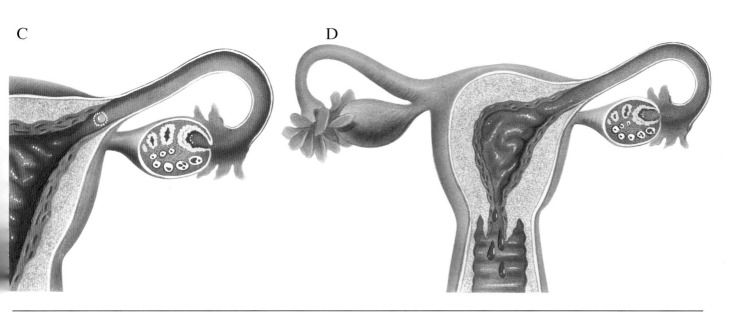

# How ova are formed

The female egg cells, the ova, develop inside the ovaries from minute immature cells. Each ovum is a tiny, specialized cell. It has only 23 chromosomes – just half as many as normal human body cells. The only other human cell with 23 chromosomes is the male sex cell, the sperm. When male and female sex cells join together they form a single cell, or zygote, with 46 chromosomes. The chromosomes carry the *genes* which hold the genetic information from the parents; this will decide how the new person will develop.

An ovum lives between 12 and 24 hours. It will live longer only if it is fertilized by a sperm.

When a girl is born, she has hundreds of thousands of immature cells in her ovaries. Most of these will not develop; only about 200 in each ovary will reach maturity and become ova.

In the ovary, each immature cell is surrounded by a round cluster of cells called a follicle. Hormones stimulate the follicles to mature, and every 28 days between puberty and the age of about 50, a mature follicle breaks and releases an ovum into the oviduct. The ova usually come from alternate ovaries. This is known as ovulation.

The broken follicle now forms a *corpus luteum*, or yellow body. It produces the hormone progesterone. If the ovum is not fertilized, within a fortnight the corpus luteum shrinks and stops producing progesterone. Menstruation begins. A fortnight later, another ovum matures, and the cycle repeats itself.

*A close-up picture of the inside of an ovary. In the walls of the ovary are clusters of cells called follicles. Inside each is an immature egg cell which is growing in size. Every 28 days, a follicle breaks open to release a mature ovum. The broken follicle forms a corpus luteum. This produces progesterone which gets the uterus ready for a fertilized egg.*

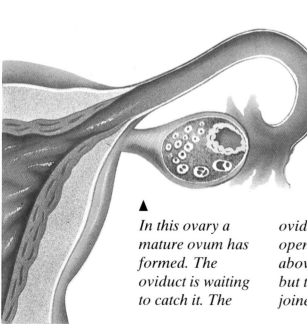

▲ *In this ovary a mature ovum has formed. The oviduct is waiting to catch it. The oviduct's fringed opening is just above the ovary, but they are not joined.*

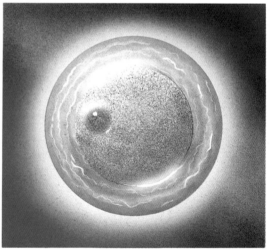

▲ *A mature ovum. Within the protective membrane is cytoplasm. The round dark blob is the cell's nucleus.*

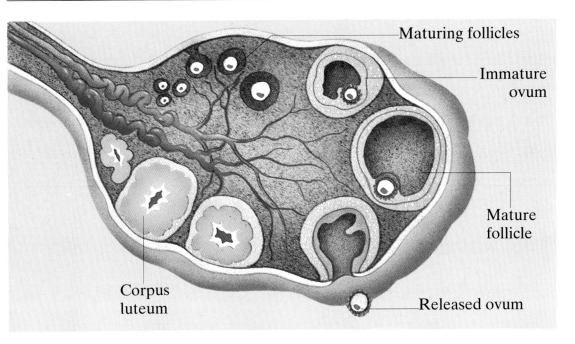

Maturing follicles

Immature ovum

Mature follicle

Corpus luteum

Released ovum

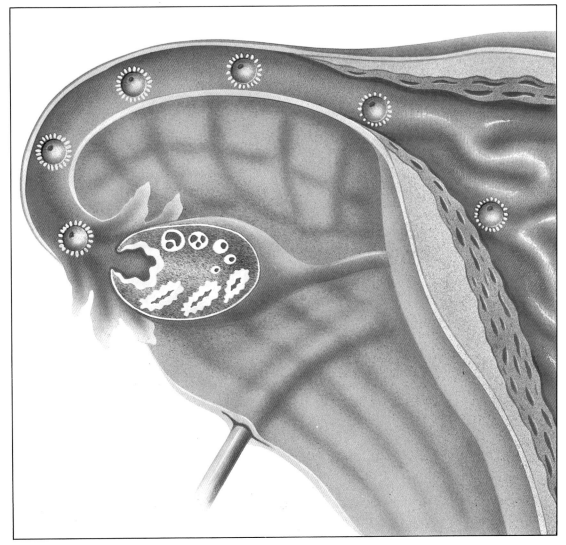

◄
*How a mature ovum makes its way from the ovary (1), down the oviduct to reach the uterus where it may develop. The endometrium, or lining of the uterus, (2) has grown thicker ready to receive a fertilized ovum.*

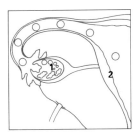

# How sperm are formed

The sperm, or male sex cell, is one of the smallest of all human cells; it is far too small to see without a microscope. The main part of a sperm is its head. This contains the nucleus, with its 23 chromosomes carrying genetic information. The head is connected by a mid-section to a long tail.

Sperm production takes about 40 days. Boys begin to produce sperm after puberty. Production takes place in the testicles. These hang outside the main part of the body so that their temperature is low enough for sperm production.

Inside the testicles, cells with 46 chromosomes divide by a complicated process called *meiosis* to form two new sex cells, each of which has only 23 chromosomes. These cells then develop into the sperm, with the nucleus in the head, and the long, mobile tail.

During *sexual intercourse*, a man releases about 400 million sperm at a time into a woman's vagina. The seminal fluid helps to protect them from acid substances there. They make their way up the woman's vagina, through the uterus and into her oviducts. They move by lashing their tails about. Most of them die on their 40-minute journey, and only about 100 arrive in her oviducts. If a sperm meets an ovum, fertilization can take place; after three days, the remaining sperm will die.

*A picture of a sperm magnified millions of times. In the head is the nucleus which contains the chromosomes. At the front is the acrosome which enables the sperm to penetrate the ovum. The mid-section contains mitochondria which create energy for the sperm to move, which it does by thrashing its tail.*
▼

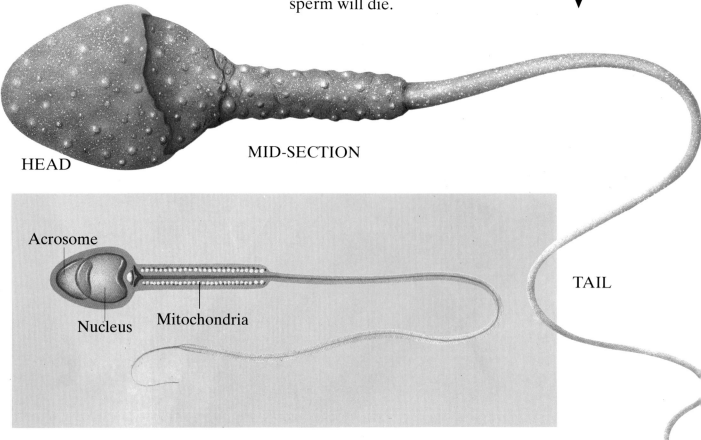

HEAD      MID-SECTION      TAIL

Acrosome

Nucleus    Mitochondria

The sperm (**1**) has managed to make its way into the ovum. The sperm and ovum join together to form a single new cell. It ◀ contains 23 chromosomes from the mother (**2**) and 23 from the father (**3**). The two sets of chromosomes pair up. The information they carry will determine all the new being's physical characteristics – its sex, its size, the colour of its eyes and so on.

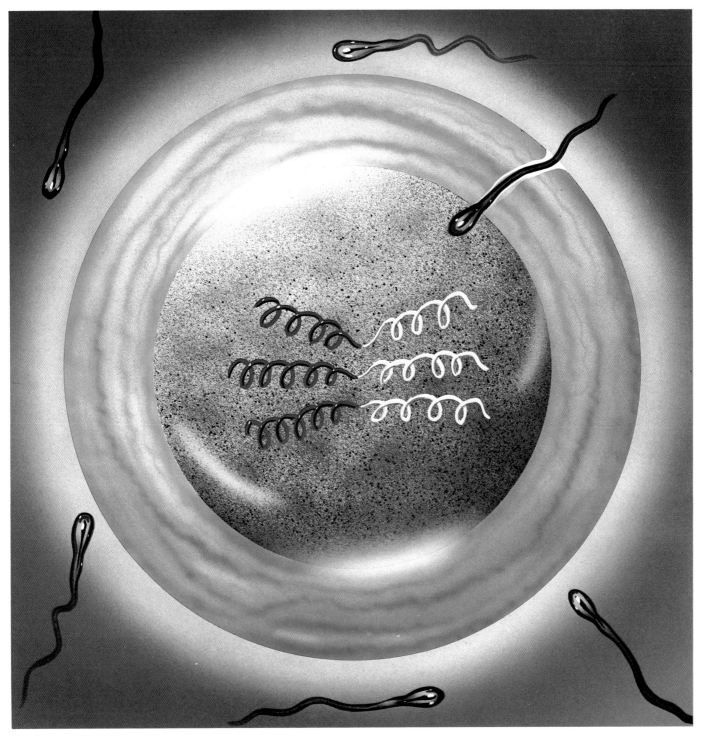

# Fertilization

Fertilization takes place when a man's sperm meets a woman's ovum. During sexual intercourse the man puts his stiffened penis into the woman's vagina and releases his semen there. Some of the millions of sperm swimming in his semen make their way through the woman's uterus into her oviducts.

An ovum can live for between 12 and 24 hours and a sperm for about three days. If during this time they meet, fertilization can take place. The head of a sperm makes its way through the outer surface of the ovum. As soon as this happens the ovum's membrane changes, and as a result no other sperm can make its way into it.

The new cell formed from the ovum and sperm is called a zygote. In it, the 23 chromosomes from the nucleus of the father's sperm join up with the 23 chromosomes from the mother's ovum to make a cell with a single nucleus containing the normal human cell number of 46 chromosomes. This is the first cell of the new being.

A few hours after it has been fertilized, the zygote divides to make two identical new cells, using a process called *mitosis*. Then each of the new cells divides into two more, forming four cells. These divide to make eight, and so on. Each cell contains exact copies of the chromosomes in the ones before; so the information stored in each cell is identical.

The cluster of cells takes about four days to move down through the oviduct to the uterus.

Centrioles

Nuclear membrane

Pairs of chromosome threads

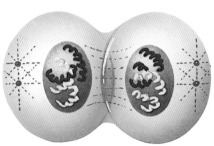

◄ *Division starts when the membrane around the cell's nucleus disappears. The chromosomes move to the centre. Structures called centrioles move to opposite sides of the cell.*

*The centrioles then send out fibres which become attached to the middle of the chromosomes which then split into two identical threads.*

*One thread from each moves to each centriole.*

*A new nuclear membrane forms round each chromosome group. Two new centrioles are formed; the cell divides into two daughter cells, exactly like the original.*

The single-celled zygote divides over and over again into 2, 4, 8, 16, 32, 64 identical cells, and so on. These are clustered together in a ball; this is known as a morula, *from the Latin word for mulberry.* ►

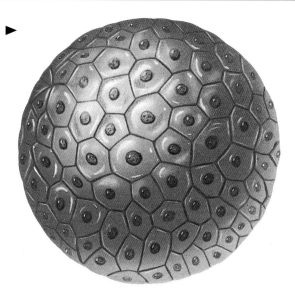

A new life begins. A mature ovum leaves the ovary (**1**). On its way down the oviduct, a sperm fertilizes it (**2**). The egg and sperm combine and the new cell divides over and over again to form a cluster of cells (**3**), ▼

which moves along the tube towards the uterus. The lining of the uterus, the endometrium (**4**), has thickened; it is ready to receive the fertilized ovum.

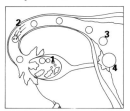

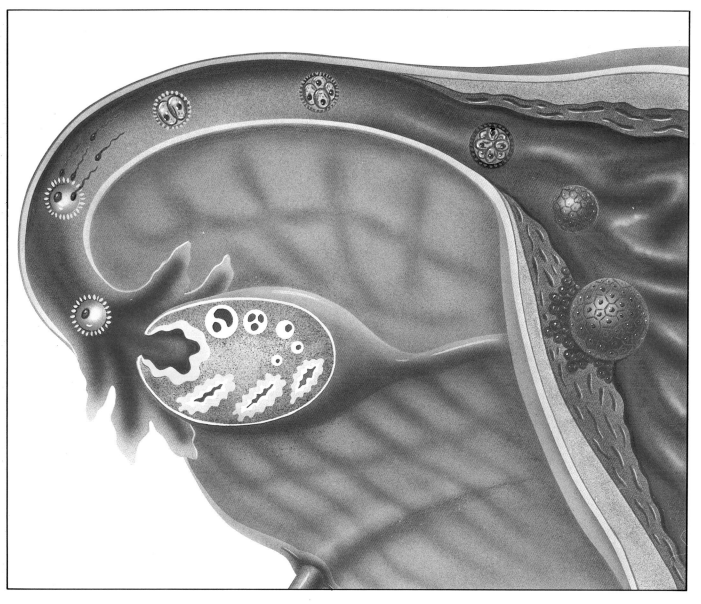

# The womb

While the cluster of cells has been dividing and travelling down to the uterus, the lining of the uterus – the endometrium – has been changing, ready to receive it. It has grown into a thick layer with a rich supply of blood vessels. The ball of cells implants itself in the lining.

If the endometrium is not ready when the cell cluster reaches it, the cells pass down through the uterus and out of the woman's body. In most cases, however, the endometrium is ready to receive the cluster of cells.

The dividing morula now forms a hollow clump of cells, just big enough to be seen. It is called a *blastocyst*. It forms tiny projections called *villi* on its outside, which burrow into the endometrium. This stage is called *implantation*, and from now on the developing cell cluster is known as an *embryo*. It stays in the uterus, and takes the nourishment and *oxygen* it needs to grow from its mother's blood supply.

From now on, the dividing cells develop in different ways. Some will become the embryo baby. Others will form the envelopes which will surround the embryo, giving it protection and nourishment. These are the *chorion* (which will produce the *placenta*) and the *amnion*.

*The zygote divides until it forms a solid cluster of cells known as a* ▼

*morula. After more cell divisions, it changes into a hollow sphere*

*(shown in the last two pictures) called a blastocyst, just big enough to see.*

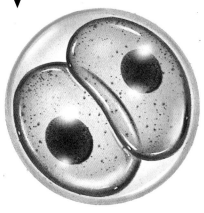
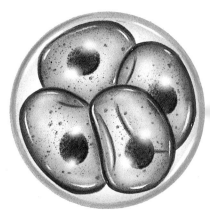
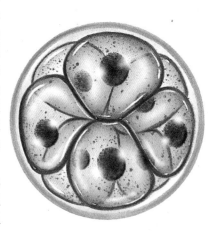
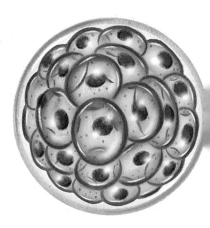
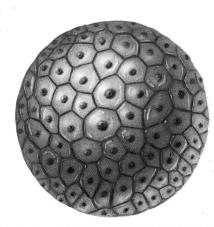
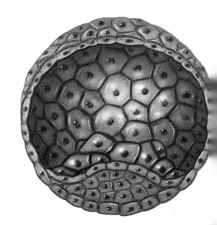

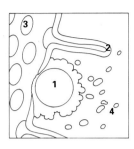

The blastocyst (**1**) arrives in the uterus (**4**) and 'burrows' into the endometrium (**2**), which has developed a layer rich in blood vessels to receive it. The uterus is normally about the size of a small pear; it has muscular walls (**3**) and is hollow inside. Its muscles are so elastic that they can stretch during a woman's pregnancy to allow room for the growing baby. After the baby is born, the muscles contract and the uterus goes back to its normal size.

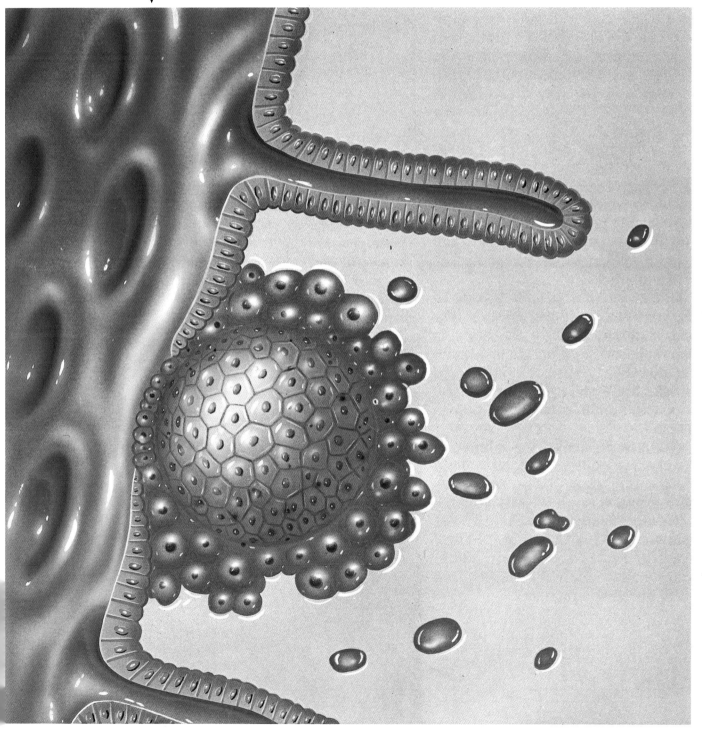

# Early days

During the second and third weeks the cluster of dividing cells, now known as the embryo, settles into place in the mother's uterus. Projections called chorionic villi make their way into the lining of the uterus and begin to take nourishment for the embryo from her blood. These villi develop into the placenta, which is connected to the embryo by the *umbilical cord*.

A membrane called the amnion develops round the embryo. This is like a bag and it fills with a liquid called *amniotic fluid*. The embryo floats safely in this. The liquid cushions it from bumps and knocks, and keeps it at a constant temperature of 37° Centigrade.

Different types of cell appear in the embryo. These will develop into such different parts of the body as skin, hair and nails, nerves and brain, the digestive system, blood vessels, muscles and bones. As *differentiation* occurs the embryo begins to change shape.

After three weeks, the embryo is about three millimetres long – about the size of a grain of rice. From now on it grows very quickly. By 28 days, it has more than doubled its size. The *amniotic sac* round it is well developed. Its heart starts to form and to beat, at first jerkily but soon with a quick but steady rhythm.

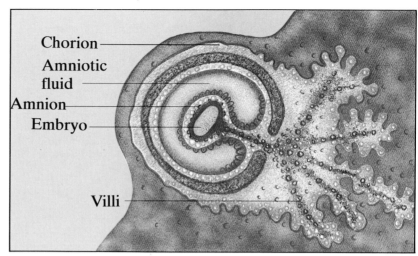

▲
*Finger-like villi reach out from the chorion into the endometrium. They take food for the embryo from the mother's blood.*

*The embryo has settled into the endometrium (A). By this time it has three distinct layers of cells. The ectoderm (B), the mesoderm (not visible) and the endoderm (C). It is protected by the amniotic fluid (E), while the chorion (D) absorbs food from the endometrium.*
▼

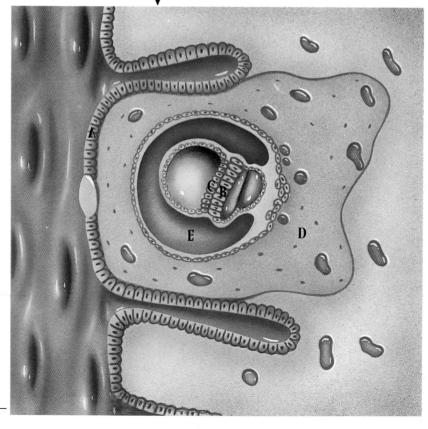

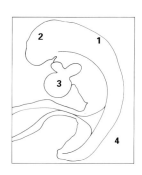

The new being is beginning to take shape. The spinal column (**1**) is already beginning to form all down its length. An arching cluster of cells at ▼ one end will develop into the head (**2**). At this stage, the heart (**3**) is just a broadening of a blood vessel which looks like a bag. The embryo is wrapped in a membrane called the amnion. This will develop into a pouch around the embryo, full of fluid. This amniotic fluid (**4**) protects the embryo from bumps and keeps it at a constant temperature. The embryo is connected to the placenta by the umbilical cord (**5**).

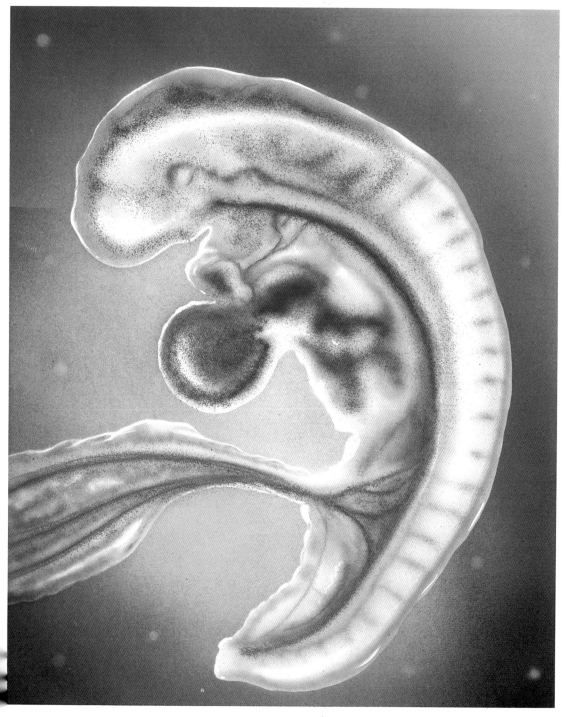

# Taking shape

Two months after fertilization, we can see that the developing embryo is a human being; it looks different from the embryo of any other animal, and the important parts of its body are forming.

At three weeks the embryo is about the size of a grain of rice. Blood cells are forming and its spine, brain and spinal cord are starting to develop. The head area is huge compared with the rest of its body. Just beneath the head area, a broadening in a blood vessel forms the beginning of the heart. It starts to beat, irregularly at first but soon steadily. The eye and ear sockets begin to form, and the amniotic sac fills with fluid.

During the fifth week, the embryo's legs and arms are forming. At first they look like buds, but soon they lengthen and in the seventh week shoulder and elbow, hip and knee joints develop. Hands and then feet form. To begin with the fingers and toes are webbed, but by the ninth week they are separate. Meanwhile, the embryo's digestive system is forming, and the lungs begin to develop in the seventh week.

All the time the embryo is growing quickly. At five weeks, it is about 10 millimetres long; at the end of the sixth week, it is 13 millimetres long. By the eighth week, it is 40 millimetres long.

By the time two months have passed, we can see the embryo's eyes, covered with a layer of skin which will form its eyelids. Its ears too have taken shape, and we can see the beginnings of a mouth. The head is bent over the body, but the neck is starting to take shape. It is beginning to move its limbs. Now we stop talking about the embryo; instead it is known as a *foetus*.

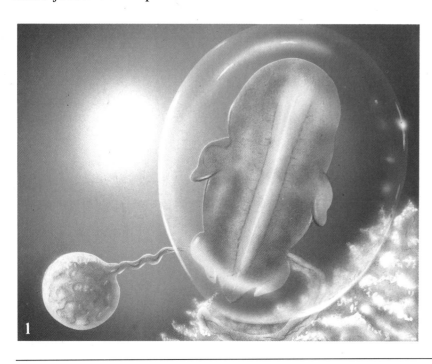

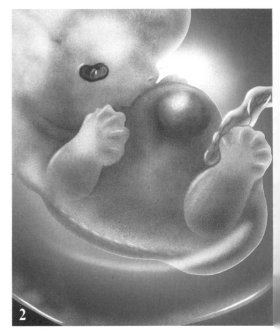

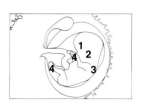

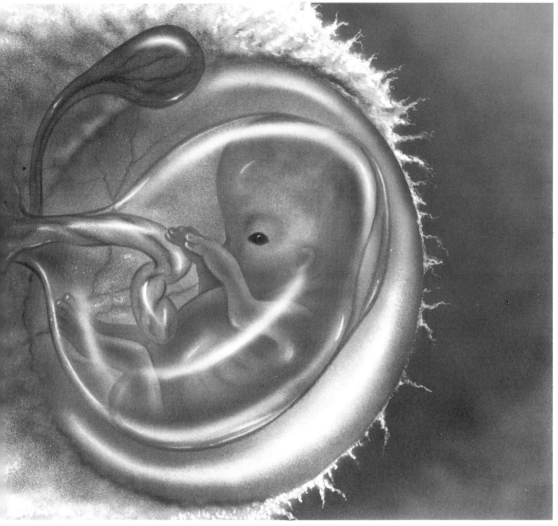

◄ *In the sixth week of the embryo's development, its eyes (1) and ears (2) begin to take shape. The head starts to stretch out from the body, and the neck (3) becomes defined. The hands and feet (4) begin to form.*

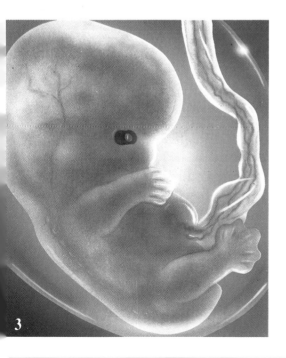

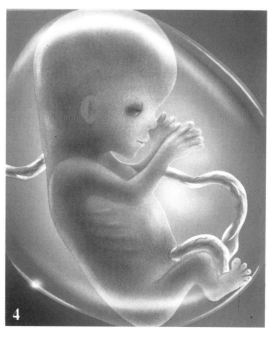

◄ *The embryo grows quickly inside the amniotic sac. The head, spine and limb buds form (1); the head is enormous compared with the rest of the body and already has eyes (2). Limbs develop joints and soon grow fingers and toes (3). After two months it is beginning to look like a tiny baby (4).*

# The baby grows

Until the end of the second month, the embryo has fitted into the hollow centre of its mother's uterus; from now on, the uterus has to stretch to make room for the foetus, its amniotic sac and the placenta. Soon the mother's abdomen will begin to swell out and her pregnancy will show more and more.

During the next weeks the foetus's inner organs grow, and its heart begins to pump blood round its body. Muscles start to form, and nails and hair grow. It moves its limbs around increasingly strongly. By week 14 it is fully formed, though very tiny; it is 12 centimetres long, and weighs 135 grams.

By week 20 the foetus is moving around so strongly that its mother can feel its movements. It can open and close its fists and its eyes, it falls asleep and wakes up frequently, and it even has hiccups! If an embryo is born after week 24, it is just possible for it to live in an *incubator*, although it weighs less than a kilogram and measures only about 30 centimetres long.

In about week 12, the mother may see an *ultrasound* picture of her baby, built up through high frequency sound waves and shown on a screen. This allows doctors to make sure that the baby is developing properly. They can also tell whether the baby will be a boy or girl.

*In the fifth month, the foetus moves about in the amniotic fluid, sucking its thumb and kicking so strongly that the mother feels the movements.*

*This six-month old foetus is floating in the amniotic fluid (1). Its organs have taken shape and now it needs to grow. Its body will take its baby shape as fat is deposited in its tissues. Until birth the umbilical cord (2) is the only source of food and oxygen available. This is the bond with the mother, from whom the foetus gets its life.*

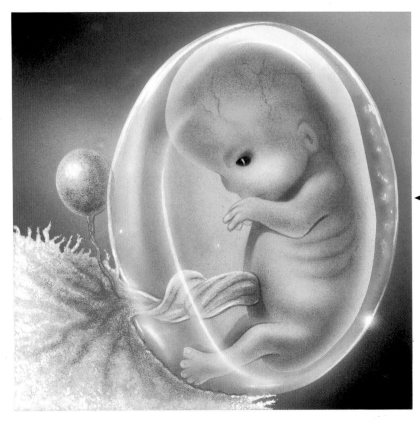

◄ *During the early weeks of a foetus's development, its head is very large in proportion to the rest of its body. The eye sockets develop in the fifth week; soon they are covered by skin, which will form the eyelids.*

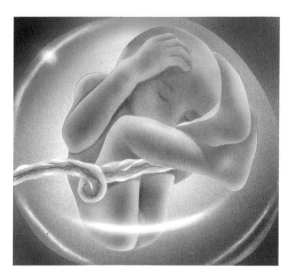

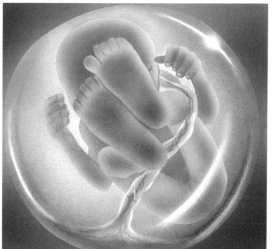

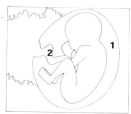

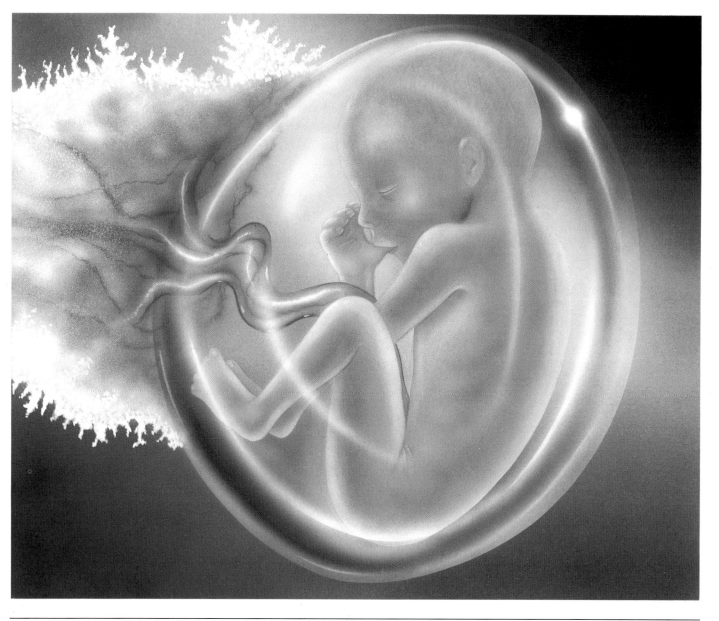

# Journey to birth

The development first of the embryo and then of the foetus is made possible by the placenta, the vital link between it and its mother.

The placenta develops from the little projections which grow from the embryo into the lining of its mother's uterus, and from blood vessels in the lining. The blood vessels from the embryo (and later foetus) and from the mother are separated by two layers of cells; between them is a space filled with the mother's blood.

The placenta is connected with the foetus through the umbilical cord, which joins it at the abdomen. Through the cord run a vein and two arteries. The umbilical arteries take fresh blood carrying oxygen and nutrients from the mother to the embryo; the umbilical vein takes back blood with *carbon dioxide* and the foetus's waste products to the placenta.

After 38 weeks, the baby is ready to be born. It usually turns so that it is head down in the pelvis. In the first stage of *labour* (as the birth process is called) the mother begins to have strong, regular muscle spasms called *contractions*. Gradually the *cervix*, the lower end of her uterus, opens wider and wider. After about 12 hours (this time can vary quite a lot) the cervix is some 10 centimetres in diameter. The second stage begins; it lasts about an hour. Even stronger contractions push the baby through the cervix, down the vagina and out of its mother's body. The umbilical cord is cut and tied to form the baby's *navel*. More contractions push out the placenta. Now the baby is ready to live in the world – though it will need care and help for many years.

*Three months after fertilization, the placenta is fully formed. The heart of the foetus pumps blood to the placenta through the umbilical cord. Two layers of cells there keep the foetus's blood separate from that of its mother, but allow waste products from the foetal blood to pass out, and oxygen and nutrients from the mother's blood to pass into the foetus's blood.*
▼

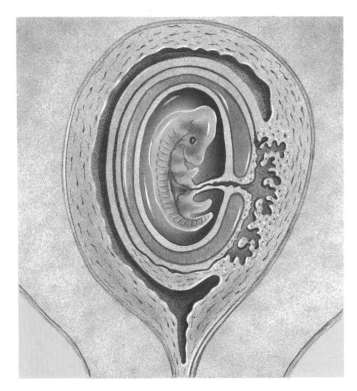

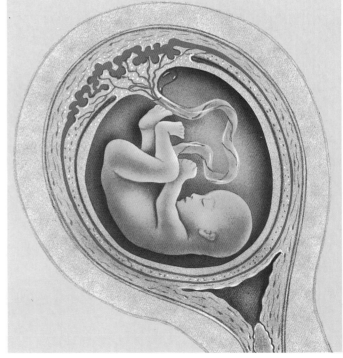

*The baby is ready to be born at 38 weeks. It must make its way out through the cervix (1) and the vagina (2). First, the membranes round the baby break, and the amniotic fluid (3) flows out.* ►

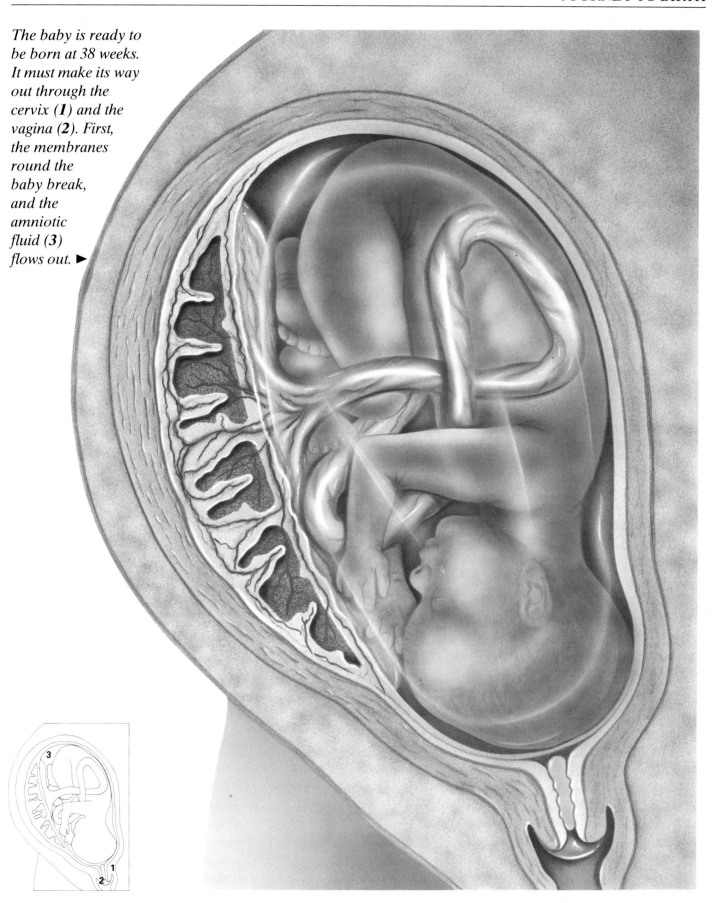

# Finding out

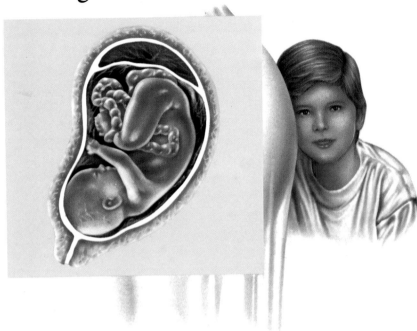

## Hearing the heartbeat

The heart of a foetus beats much more rapidly than your own heart or the heart of a grown-up person. If a member of your family, or a very close friend, is in the later months of pregnancy, you may be able to hear this for yourself.

To do so, you will need a watch with a second hand. Using this, take the pulse of the pregnant woman, and count how many times her heart beats during one minute. Write this down.

Now place your ear slightly below the centre of her abdomen. You will be able to hear the heart of the foetus. When you count the beats, you will find there are about 250 a minute. Compare the two figures, and see how different they are.

## Boy or girl?

Why do some embryos develop into boys and others into girls? The answer lies in the information on the embryo's chromosomes. These are the thread-like structures in the nucleus of its cells, 23 of which originally came from its father and 23 from its mother. Most of the chromosomes can be paired together but two – the ones that determine our sex – can be different. Every woman has two X chromosomes in this last couple, while every man has one X chromosome, and one Y chromosome.

A man can pass either an X chromosome or a Y chromosome on to his children; a woman can pass on only an X chromosome. Any embryo with a Y chromosome will develop into a male.

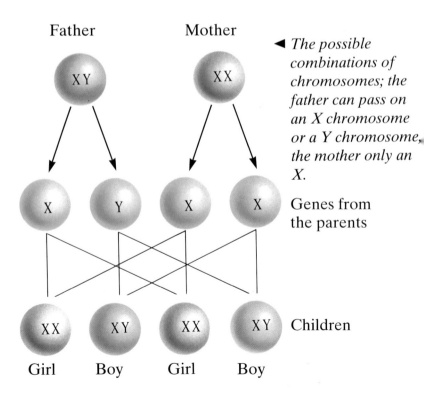

*◄ The possible combinations of chromosomes; the father can pass on an X chromosome or a Y chromosome, the mother only an X.*

## The laws of heredity

How we develop is ruled by our genes. These are instructions carried on the chromosomes we inherit from our parents, which control the way in which our bodies will take shape.

We carry a complete set of instructions from each of our parents. In many cases one instruction is stronger, or more *dominant*, than the other, *recessive* gene. The gene for dark hair, for instance, is a dominant gene, and that for fair hair is recessive. This means that a person who inherits one gene for dark hair and one for fair hair will have dark hair. Sometimes neither gene is dominant.

*The genes for hair colour are passed on from parents to their children. The dark genes are dominant. Two fair-haired people can only produce a fair-haired child. A dark-haired father and a fair-haired mother will have a dark-haired child if ▶ the father has passed on his dark gene. But he may have a fair-haired recessive gene, masked by the dark one. If he passes this on, he can produce a fair-haired child.*

| Characteristic | Father's family | | | Mother's family | | |
|---|---|---|---|---|---|---|
| | Father | Grandpa | Grandma | Mother | Grandpa | Grandma |
| Colour of hair | fair | fair | fair | dark | dark | fair |
| Wavy or straight | straight | straight | curly | curly | curly | straight |
| Colour of eyes | blue | blue | brown | brown | brown | blue |
| Shape of nose | pointed | pointed | upturned | button | button | pointed |
| Shape of lips | broad | thin | broad | thin | broad | thin |
| Size of ears | small | large | small | large | small | small |

◀ *Make a chart like this one with details of your family. How do your features compare? Make a chart that shows the characteristics you and your brothers and sisters have inherited from your parents.*

# Index and glossary

Puberty 6,10,12,14
*The time in the body's development when the reproductive glands and organs start to mature. It usually occurs between 11 and 14 in girls, and 14 and 16 in boys. Puberty marks the beginning of adolescence.*

Recessive 29
*The term describing a gene whose influence can be overridden by a more dominant gene.*

Reproduction 4,17
*The process in which a new being is formed by the joining of male and female sex cells.*

Reproductive cycle 10

Reproductive system, female 6,7

Reproductive system, male 8,9

Scrotum 8,16
*The pouch of skin containing a man's testicles.*

Semen 8,16
*The fluid from a man's testicles and prostate containing his sperm.*

Seminal fluid 8,14
*Another name for semen.*

Seminiferous tubules 8,9
*The coiled tubes in a man's testicles where sperm are produced.*

Sex cells 4,12,14
*Male or female reproductive cells; male cells are the sperm, the female cells the ova.*

Sex characteristics 6,8
*The bodily characteristics which are different in men and women. In men these include testicles, a penis and a prostate gland. Men also have deep voices, beards and hairy bodies. Women have ovaries, a uterus and breasts. Their voices remain high and they have less facial and body hair than men.*

Sexual intercourse 14,16
*The reproductive process in which a man's erect (stiffened) penis enters a woman's vagina, and releases semen.*

Shoulder joints 22
Shoulders 10
Size 15
Skin 10,20
Sperm 4,9,10,14-17
*The male reproductive cell (also called a spermatozoon).*

Spermatozoon See Sperm
Spinal column 21
Spinal cord 22
Spine 22
Teeth 4
Testicles 8-10,14
*Two glands contained in a man's scrotum which produce sperm and male sex hormones.*

Testosterone 8
*A hormone produced in the testicles which controls a man's secondary sex characteristics.*

Thumb sucking 24
Tissues 24
Ultrasound 24
*A scanning technique used during pregnancy to check on the foetus's development.*

Umbilical arteries 26
Umbilical cord 20,21,24,26
*This tube connects the unborn baby to the mother's placenta. Through its blood vessels, the baby receives nutrients and gets rid of waste. After birth the tube is tied and cut. The remains of it form the navel, or belly-button.*

Umbilical vein 26
Urethra 8,9
*The tube leading from the bladder through which urine leaves the body; it passes through a man's penis. When this becomes erect the opening from the bladder is shut off, and semen passes out of his body through the urethra.*

Urine 8
Uterus 6,7,10-14,16-20,24,26
*Also known as the womb, this is the hollow muscular organ in a woman's body where the developing embryo grows.*

Vagina 6-8,10,14,16,26,27
*The passage leading from the cervix to the outside of a woman's body.*

Vas deferens 8,9
*The duct taking sperm and secretions out of the testicle.*

Villi 18,20
*Tiny finger-like projections, like those found on the outside of the chorion.*

Womb See Uterus
Yellow body See Corpus lutem
Zygote 4,12,16,17
*The cell formed when a sperm and ovum unite.*

# THE GLOW IN THE DARK

# BOOK OF

# SPACE

Nicholas Harris

*illustrated by*
Sebastian Quigley

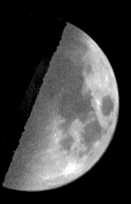

*orpheus*

Meteors

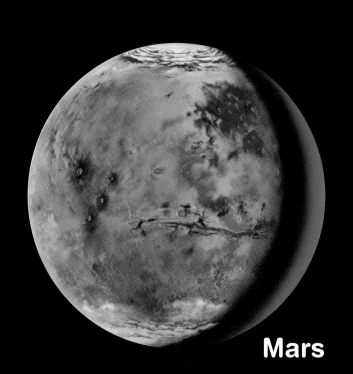

Mars

# CONTENTS

**W**E THINK of space as the vast, dark expanse beyond our own planet Earth. The Sun's light fills the sky by day, of course, but at night other objects in space become visible: stars, the Milky Way, the Moon, shooting stars, and so on. We can see these objects because they glow, either with their own light, or with light reflected from the Sun. This book also shows objects in space that glow. For the pages with special glow-in-the-dark text and illustrations, look for the pink corner squares. Hold the book open at any one of these pages under a light for twenty seconds or so, then turn out the light. Have fun!

Milky
Way
Galaxy

# ABOUT THIS BOOK

Planet

Comet

Moon

**L**OOK UP at the sky on a clear night. What is the brightest thing you can see? On many nights it will be the Moon. It looks so large and bright because it is our nearest neighbour in space.

Stars may look tiny, but in fact they are all gigantic, thousands of times the size of Earth!

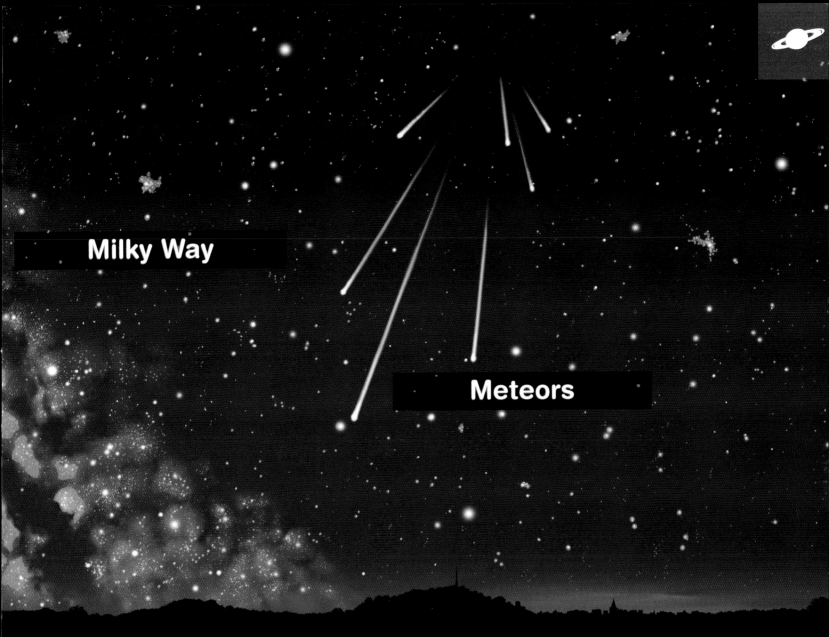

**Milky Way**

**Meteors**

All the stars we can see belong to the Milky Way Galaxy. From Earth, our view of one of the Galaxy's spiral arms looks like a misty band across the heavens, the "milky way" from which the Galaxy takes its name.

Sometimes, you may be able to catch sight of a comet hanging in the sky. Look out, too, for meteors or "shooting stars", split-second streaks of light. They are tiny fragments burning up high above Earth.

**T**HE SUN is one of billions of stars that make up the Galaxy. Like all stars, it is a giant, spinning ball of very hot gas. It produces massive amounts of energy at its core.

The surface of the Sun bubbles and spits like water boiling in a pan. Huge flares and arches of glowing gas sometimes burst into space. Sunspots, dark, cooler areas, appear on the Sun's surface from time to time.

**Arch**

**Jupiter**
*(to scale)*

**Earth**
*(to scale)*

**Flare**

# THE SUN

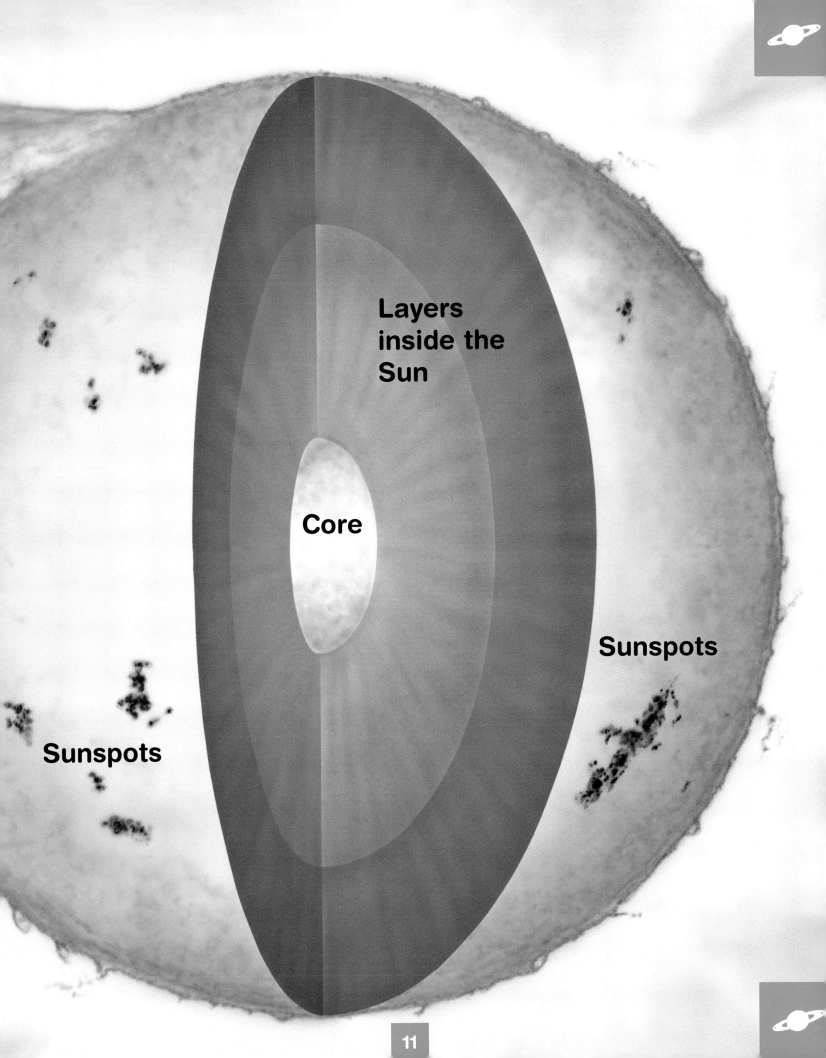

Layers
inside the
Sun

Core

Sunspots

Sunspots

THIS IS what the Milky Way Galaxy would look like if we zoomed out into space and looked back down at it. It is a gigantic mass of stars. The swirling pattern the stars make is called a spiral. The Galaxy has a bulge at its centre. Our Sun is just one of the billions of stars in the Milky Way Galaxy. It is found on one of the spiral "arms", just over halfway out from the centre.

## OUR GALAXY, A SPIRAL OF STARS

**Venus**

**Mercury**

**Earth**

**Mars**

**Jupiter**

**H**ERE, the planets of the Solar System are drawn to scale. Jupiter is the largest planet. It is more massive than all the others combined.

The four inner planets are Mercury, Venus, Earth and Mars. They are mostly made of rock.

Sun
Mercury
Venus
Earth
Mars

Asteroids

Jupiter

Saturn

Uranus

The inner planets are dwarfed by four outer planets, the "gas giants" Jupiter, Saturn, Uranus and Neptune. They are mostly made of gas. Pluto is the odd one out. A small outer planet, it is made of ice and rock.

The diagram below, also drawn to scale, shows the distance each planet lies from the Sun.

**Uranus**

**Saturn**

**Neptune**

**Pluto**

# THE PLANETS TO SCALE

**Pluto**
*(when nearest the sun)*
**Neptune**

**Pluto**

**T**HE SOLAR SYSTEM consists of the Sun, its family of nine planets and their moons, comets, asteroids, meteoroids and vast amounts of gas.

All these objects, large or small, travel around, or orbit, the Sun.

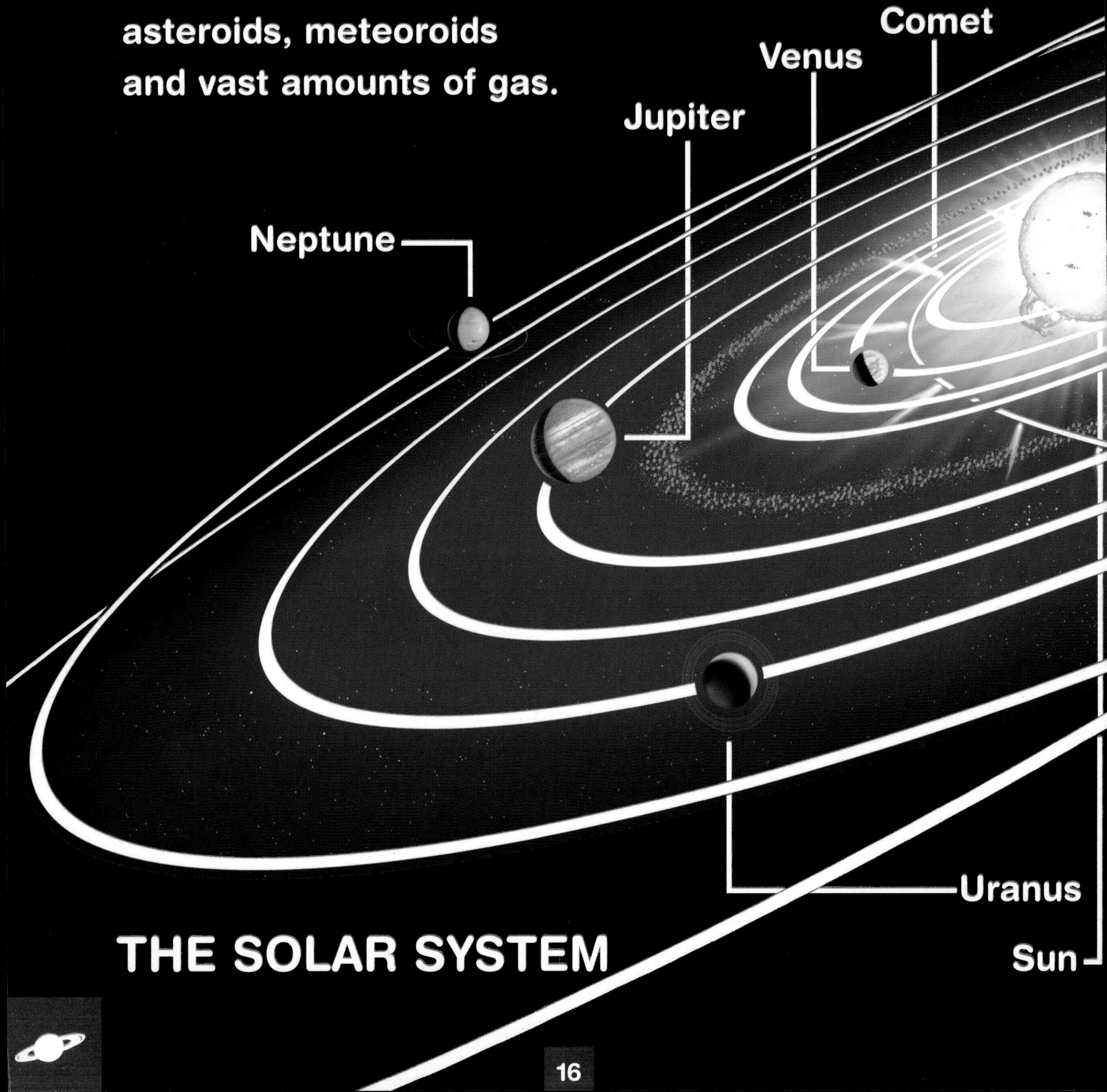

Comet

Venus

Jupiter

Neptune

Uranus

# THE SOLAR SYSTEM

Sun

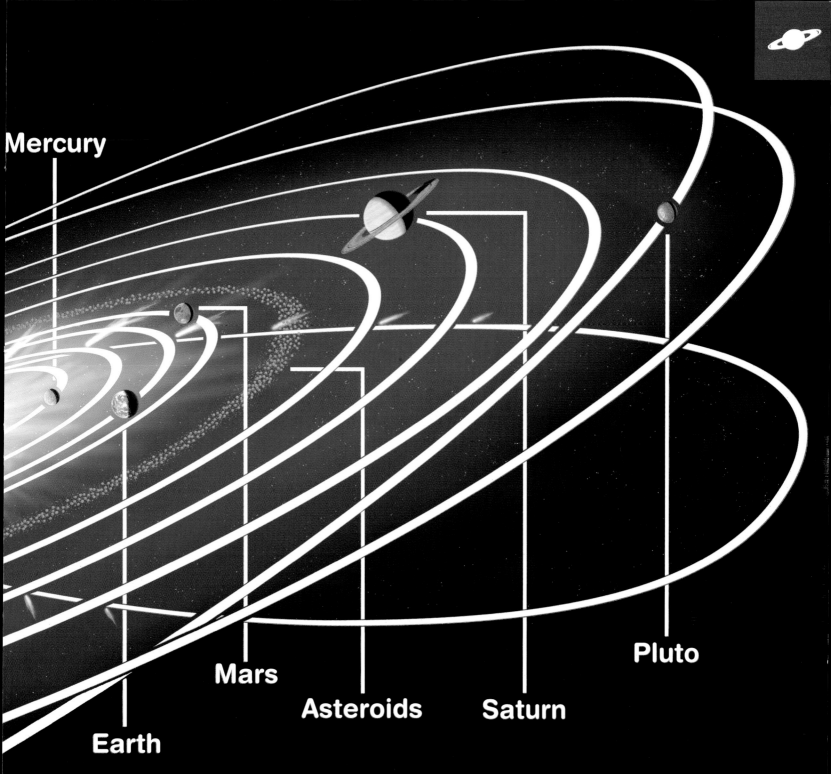

Mercury

Mars

Earth

Asteroids

Saturn

Pluto

The planets orbit the Sun in the same direction (anticlockwise on the illustration). For part of its journey around the Sun, Pluto lies inside Neptune's orbit. Many comets loop in towards the Sun from distant parts of the Solar System.

Mercury

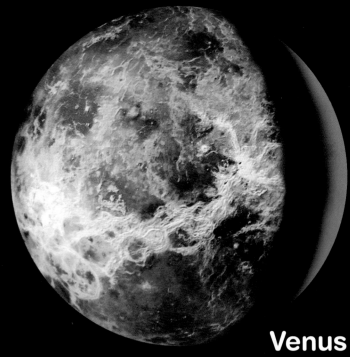

Venus

**M**ERCURY is the nearest planet to the Sun. During the day it is extremely hot. But at night it is bitterly cold.

**V**ENUS is covered in thick clouds of deadly acid. On its surface, the temperature is hot enough to melt lead.

**E**ARTH is the only planet to have liquid water, vital for any life to exist. The atmosphere protects us from the Sun's harmful rays.

## THE INNER PLANETS

Earth

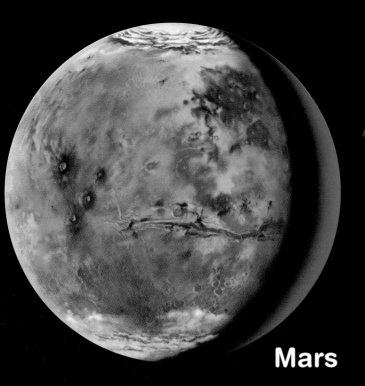

Mars

**Asteroids**

**M**ARS is the "Red Planet", so-called because of the colour of the dust that blankets its surface. Now completely barren, Mars may once have had running water. Some scientists think that there could have been life on Mars in the past. The only water on the Martian surface today is frozen at the polar icecaps.

**A**STEROIDS are small blocks of rock and metal. Most are found in a belt between Mars and Jupiter. Meteoroids, fragments of asteroids, sometimes come near Earth. Comets are lumps of dust and rock frozen together. Long tails of gas and dust are swept back by the Sun's rays.

Comet

THE MOON is a ball of rock that orbits the Earth. All the planets, except for Mercury and Venus, have moons. Our Moon is a barren world pitted with craters. These have been blasted out by rocks crashing down from space, called meteorites. There is no atmosphere on the Moon.

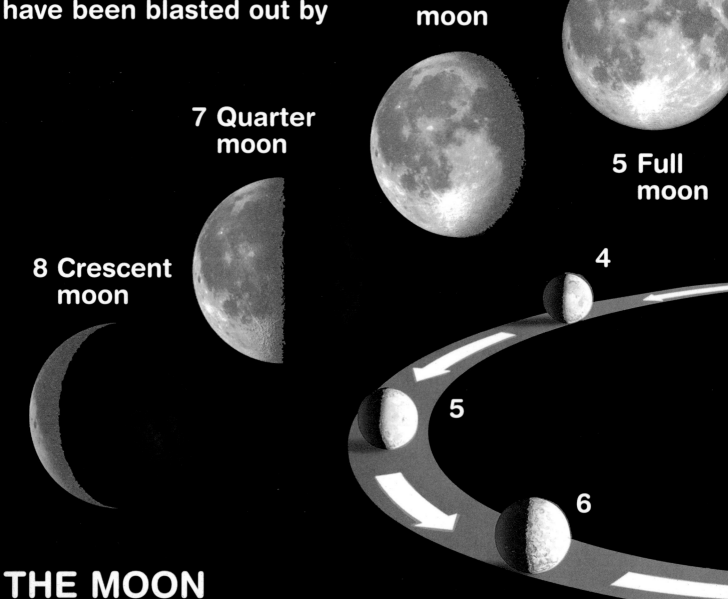

6 Gibbous moon

7 Quarter moon

5 Full moon

8 Crescent moon

4

5

6

# THE MOON

**4 Gibbous moon**

**3 Quarter moon**

**2 Crescent moon**

**1 New moon**

The shape of the Moon seems to change slightly each night *(above).* This is because the same side always faces us as the Moon orbits Earth *(below).* It is our view of the sunlit part that changes.

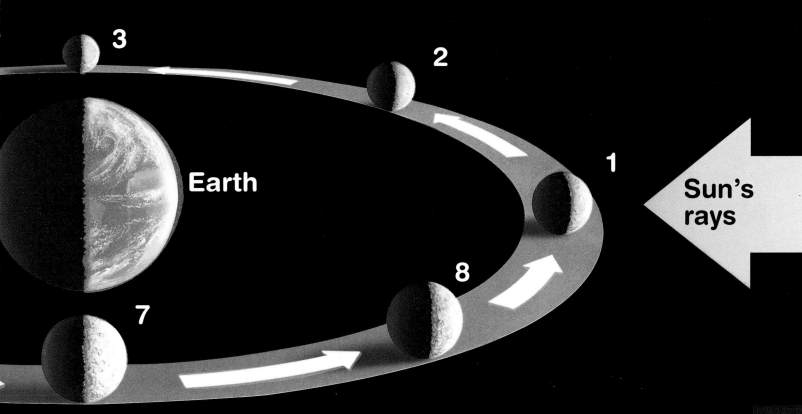

3

2

Earth

1

Sun's rays

8

7

Jupiter

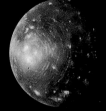

**Ganymede**     **Callisto**

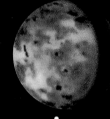

**Io**          **Europa**

**J**UPITER is large enough to contain 1300 Earths. Its patterns of red, yellow and white are produced by high-speed winds. The Great Red Spot is a giant storm. Jupiter's four largest moons *(above right)* are called the "Galileans".

**S**ATURN is famous for its rings. They are made of billions of blocks of ice and rock. Saturn's largest moon, Titan, is the only moon in the Solar System to have a thick atmosphere.

Saturn

Titan

# THE OUTER PLANETS

Triton

Uranus

Neptune

**U**RANUS, the
third gas giant,
orbits the Sun lying
almost on its side. The
other planets orbit in a
near-vertical position.
Uranus has 11 faint rings
and a family of 21 moons.

**N**EPTUNE is a bright
blue globe with a few
wispy clouds and,
occasionally, dark spots.
It has very faint rings.
Neptune's largest moon,
Triton, is the coldest
world in the Solar System.

Charon

**P**LUTO is the coldest,
smallest and most
distant planet in the
Solar System. Its moon,
Charon, is half its size.

Pluto

**Y**EARS AGO, people saw patterns of stars in the night sky. They imagined their shapes to

# CONSTELLATIONS

SOUTHERN HEMISPHERE

Pisces

Cetus

Aquarius

Eridanus

Sculptor

Phoenix

Grus

Capricornus

Fornax

Tucana

Aquila

Lepus

Reticulum

Sagittarius

Columba

Dorado

Pavo

Orion

Octans

Scorpius

Canis Major

Carina

Crux

Ophiuchus

Vela

Monoceros

Puppis

Centaurus

Lupus

Pyxis

Libra

Hydra

Corvus

Crater

Virgo

Sextans

look like gods, heroes or animals from legends. These star patterns are called constellations.

Being able to recognize constellations helps us to find stars, galaxies and other heavenly bodies.

**E**VERYTHING that we know exists—stars, rocks, animals, people, air—all belong to the Universe. Nearly all matter is contained in galaxies *(below)*.

The Universe probably came into being about 15 billion years ago. There was a massive explosion called the Big Bang. All matter, energy, space—and time itself—were created in the Big Bang.

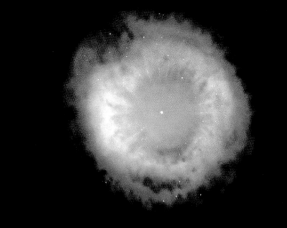

As the Universe expanded, the first stars were formed. Many, like our Sun, will shine on for billions of years. But eventually they will swell into red giants before flaking away into space, A planetary nebula is all that will remain *(above)*. A massive star will grow into a supergiant before exploding in a supernova (the remains of one are pictured *below)*.

# THE UNIVERSE

After a supernova, what is left of the old star may shrink to a tiny point. Around it, the force of gravity is so strong that nothing, not even light, can escape from it. We call these places black holes. Anything lying close to them, like the blue star shown in this illustration *(below),* will be dragged in!

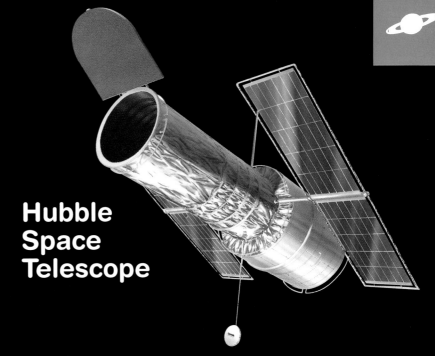

**Hubble Space Telescope**

Distances are so great in space that we have to use a special measure for them: a light year. This is the distance that light, which moves at about 300,000 kilometres per second, travels in one year. Proxima Centauri, the nearest star to us (apart from the Sun), is 4.2 light years away. The most distant objects we know are more than 13 billion light years away!

**ASTEROID** A small rocky body that orbits the Sun.

**BIG BANG** The explosion in which the Universe was created.

**BLACK HOLE** A region of space from which nothing, not even light, can escape.

**COMET** An lump of dust, ice and rock that orbits the Sun *(below)*. When it nears the Sun, long tails stream away from it.

# USEFUL WORDS

**CONSTELLATION** A pattern of stars in the night sky.

**CRATER** A saucer-shaped feature found on the surface of some planets, moons and asteroids.

**ECLIPSE** The movement of a planet or moon in front of another, or in front of the Sun.

**GALAXY** An enormous cluster of stars, gas, dust and planets *(far right)*.

**GRAVITY** The force that attracts all objects to each other. Gravity is the force that keeps the planets orbiting the Sun.

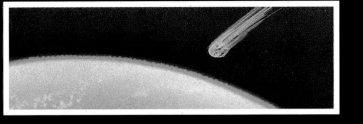

**METEORITE** A meteoroid that falls from space onto a planet or moon *(above)*.

**METEOROID** A piece of rock or dust that hurtles through the Solar System. When a meteoroid burns up close to Earth it is known as a **METEOR**.

**ORBIT** The circular or oval-shaped path followed by one object around another in space.

**PLANET** A world that orbits a star. It does not produce its own light.

**SOLAR SYSTEM** The Sun, the planets and their moons, comets, asteroids, meteoroids, dust and gas.

**STAR** A globe of gas (eg. the Sun) that produces energy inside its core.

**SUPERNOVA** The massive explosion of a supergiant star.

**UNIVERSE** All matter and space.

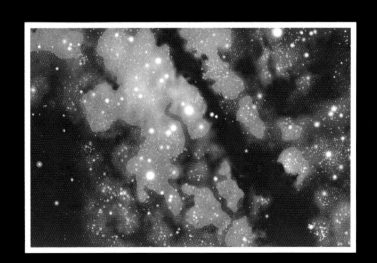

| PLANET | DIAMETER | DAY measured in Earth days or hours | YEAR measured in Earth days or years | AVERAGE DISTANCE FROM SUN | SURFACE TEMPERATURE | MOONS |
|---|---|---|---|---|---|---|
| Mercury | 4878 km | 58.6 days | 88 days | 58 million km | -170 to +350°C | none |
| Venus | 12,103 km | 243 days | 225 days | 108 million km | 490°C | none |
| Earth | 12,756 km | 23 hrs 56 min | 365.26 days | 149.6 million km | -70 to +55°C | 1 |
| Mars | 6794 km | 24.6 hours | 687 days | 228 million km | -137 to +26°C | 2 |
| Jupiter | 142,884 km | 9.8 hours | 11.8 years | 778 million km | -150°C | 28 |
| Saturn | 120,536 km | 10.2 hours | 29.4 years | 1427 million km | -180°C | 30 |
| Uranus | 51,118 km | 17.2 hours | 84 years | 2869 million km | -210°C | 21 |
| Neptune | 50,538 km | 16.1 hours | 164.8 years | 4497 million km | -220°C | 8 |
| Pluto | 2324 km | 6.4 days | 248 years | 5906 million km | -220°C | 1 |